LEARN TO DO

Hand Quilting

IN JUST ONE DAY

by Nancy Brenan Daniel

Bobbie Matela, Managing Editor
Carol Wilson Mansfield, Art Director
Linda Causee, Editor
Meredith Montross, Associate Editor
Christina Wilson, Assistant Editor
Graphic Solutions, inc-chgo, Book Design

**For a full-color catalog including books
on quilting, write to:**

**American School of Needlework®
Consumer Division
1455 Linda Vista Drive
San Marcos, CA 92069**

©1996 by Nancy Brenan Daniel.
Published by American School of Needlework®, Inc.; ASN Publishing, 1455 Linda Vista Drive, San Marcos, CA 92069

INTRODUCTION

The idea of hand quilting steps beyond the simple utility of stitching together the three layers of a quilt. The art of hand quilting endures because nothing can duplicate the look of fine hand quilting.

The first hand quilting I ever noticed was being done on a quilt mounted in a large "four-square" frame. I was about three or four at the time and on an outing with my Grandmother Ritzenthaler. Many of the other women around the frame were some kind of relation to us, but I was the only child present. Grandma had taken a hot dish to share. There were lots of treats to eat. I remember the smell of food, a nap close to the frame, a pasteboard candy box with cardboard cut-out shapes—different from the one my Grandma had at her house—and hands—hands under the frame and hands on top of the frame. After that time, I remember Grandma letting me sort the cardboard templates that she had stored in her dining room china cabinet, and I remember watching her hand quilt as I rearranged the treasured cardboard pieces from one candy box to another. All this was observed as I was sitting beneath the quilting frame my Grandfather had made her.

I hand quilted my first large quilt after I married. The quilt was an ugly disaster. The top was made of six-inch-square fabric scraps set in no particular design. I used a percale sheet, a wedding gift, for the back of the quilt. I didn't want to buy quilting thread, so I doubled #50 mercerized cotton thread. I didn't even know about between needles, so I used large-eyed embroidery needles. It seems that I remembered only two important things about my Grandma's hand quilting. She used an awful

Grandma Mary Talkington Ritzenthaler

cotton batting and I knew I didn't want that, so I bought a polyester batting. And, I remembered the way her hands moved above and below the quilt.

What did my Grandma have to say about my first effort? She loved it. She had several suggestions: Use cotton muslin sheets for the back of my quilts, use quilting thread and between needles, and keep practicing. Thank you Grandma, I have been.

Beyond all the technical aspects of hand quilting, there lies in the soul of a dedicated hand quilter, a reverence for the history and tradition of the quilt. It is a love of hand needlework as a connection to our past, and for some of us, those we love. Does that mean I think machine-quilted quilts are second rate—absolutely not! Smart quilters have used the sewing machine for piecing, appliqué and quilting ever since it came into common use. Today, most quilters save hand quilting for their finest patchwork and appliqué projects. I call these projects love tokens.

This book is meant as a technical guide to replicate a nineteenth-century-style hand quilting technique. Quilters wanting some tips and answers about improving their own technique will find many helpful suggestions. I emphasize non-stress positioning of the quilting hands for maximum efficiency and painless hand quilting—except for the occasional, too enthusiastic, needle prick.

SUPPLIES

Batting

A wide choice of batting is available for today's hand quilter. Cotton and wool battings are still used and much improved over those our great-grandmothers used. Polyester battings, in various thicknesses, are a welcome addition to the tradition of hand quilting. All types of batting are available in pre-cut bed sizes. Many shops sell premium battings that are custom cut from large rolls.

Today, most battings are of uniform thickness, easy to quilt and launder well after adequate quilting. How you choose from so many wonderful battings will depend on your experience, how much hand quilting you plan to do and how the hand-quilted project will be used when completed.

It makes sense to buy the best quality of batting you can afford when planning to hand quilt. Hand quilting is an enjoyable experience and selecting the right batting is essential.

Make a checklist of your requirements before you shop for your batting by asking yourself these questions:

1. How much hand quilting am I willing to do?

2. How will this quilt be used?

3. How often can I expect this quilt to be washed?

Your list of batting requirements might also include: easy to needle; easy to layer; washable, using manufacturers' directions; a soft drape; and non-allergenic (when that may be a concern). Avoid thick or stiff bats for your hand-quilting projects. Some very stiff resin-coated batting manufactured for the upholstery industry is sold, off the roll, as quilt batting—be aware!

Like any consumer, you will need to read the product guidelines-for-use as written by the manufacturers. Familiarize yourself with the terms used on batting labels.

Fibers Used for Quilt Batting

COTTON
Cotton batting is white or natural in color and is washable with adequate quilting. Batting that is 100% unbleached can leave stains on light-colored fabric due to the natural "litter" left in the batting. Pre-treating is suggested, but follow manufacturer's directions carefully. Batting that is 100% bleached does not have to be pre-treated except to avoid shrinkage after quilting. Fiber migration (bearding) can be a problem with untreated cotton batting, therefore, look for products with finishes that inhibit fiber migration.

Quilts with cotton batting require hand quilting at small intervals to prevent lumps after washing. Use a very sharp needle to reduce needle drag.

WOOL
Wool batting is natural in color and is washable with adequate quilting and caution. It may require extra care to prevent batting fiber migration (bearding) since wool fibers can easily twist around the quilting thread and follow it through the quilting.

Quilts with wool batting are very easy to hand quilt.

SYNTHETICS
Synthetic battings are white or dark gray in color and are very washable with adequate quilting. Polyester battings have the widest variety of sizes and thicknesses (loft). Lower loft synthetics are easy to hand quilt.

Some longer fiber synthetics migrate easily causing unsightly pilling. Look for products with finishes that inhibit fiber migration.

SILK
Silk batting is white or natural in color and washable with adequate quilting and caution. It has limited availability and use, but is very easy to hand quilt. Long fibers migrate easily causing an unsightly "bloom" or halo effect.

BLENDS
There are battings available that are blends of different fibers. Read the product label for particular information.

Special Treatment of Fibers for Batting

UNBONDED
An unbonded batting is a batting that has not been treated. Do not pre-wash or soak unbonded bats before quilting. Layering is moderate to difficult. Hand quilting with unbonded batting is very easy.

BONDED

A bonded batting is a batting that has been treated. Various finishes or heat-settings are applied to batting to prevent stretching and separation. Batting layers can be separated. Layering is moderately easy. Ease of hand quilting with a bonded batting depends on the bonding treatment.

NEEDLEPUNCHED

Batting is needlepunched to integrate fibers creating a dense, firm fiber batting. It is traditionally low-loft, not fluffy. The batting cannot be separated. Layering is very easy. Hand quilting with needlepunched batting is moderate to easy depending on fiber type.

SCRIM OR SUB-STRAIT

Fine scrim (mesh), sometimes the same fiber as the batting, is imbedded in the batting. It is usually a traditional-looking low-loft batting that cannot be separated. Layering is very easy. Hand quilting with a scrim batting is easy to difficult depending on fiber content.

Preparing the Batting for Hand Quilting

Remove batting from packaging the day before you intend to layer your quilt. The batting needs to breathe and fluff after being restricted in a bag or on a roll. Most batts will have wrinkles or folds that may need to be coaxed flat. I usually drape the batting over my large kitchen table and give it a gentle water spritz and pat the wrinkles flat. Avoid using an iron. Save and file the batting packaging.

Some battings may need washing, soaking or other preparation for hand quilting. Read and follow the manufacturers' recommendations. I always wonder if doing these preparations are necessary. But, I know that the first time I don't, there will be a disaster!

True confessions: I've soaked cotton battings until they have become cotton pulp suitable for making paper or for birds' nests; I've washed and agitated some scrim-based battings to the point of batting extinction and the birth of a fiber mass only good for camouflage material in a snow storm. You don't need to go there, I've been there and it's not pleasant and it was all my own doing. Please read and follow the manufacturers' recommendations.

Batting Chart

The batting selection chart lists most readily available battings suitable for hand quilting by fiber content and by manufacturer. The chart also indicates the maximum interval between lines of quilting as suggested by the manufacturer.

POLYESTER	COTTON & COTTON BLENDS	WOOL

Air-Lite
Poly-Insulate 6"
Simplicity™
   (Bond tight) 6+"
	Fairfield
	Cotton Classic® 4"-6"
	   (80% cotton, 20% poly)
	Soft Touch® 2"
		Hobbs
		Heirloom® Premium 3"
		
		Warm Products
		Wool Naturally™ 8"-10"

Fairfield
Traditional 4"-6"
Low-Loft® 4"-6"
Extra-Loft® 4"-6"
	Hobbs
	Heirloom®Premium 3"
	100% Organic Cotton
	   (with scrim 10",
	   without scrim 2")	

Hobbs
Poly-down® 9"
Thermore® 9"
	Morning Glory
	Clearly Cotton 4"-6"
	   (without scrim)
	"Old Fashion" Cotton 4"-6"
	   (with scrim)	

Morning Glory Glory Bee I 3"-6" Glory Bee II 8"-10" Quilter's Choice 2"-4" Great Glory 2"-4" (Dacron)	**Mountain Mist** Bleached Cotton 1/4"-1/2" Blue Ribbon 1 1/2"-2"	
Mountain Mist Quality Polyester 3" Quilt Light® 3" Designers' Choice 5"	**Warm Products** Warm & Natural™ 8"-10"	

5

Marking Tools

If you eavesdrop on a group of hand quilters, you will most likely hear heated conversations about, if not arguments about, quilt marking tools. Quilters hold very strong opinions about markers. There are some general marker guidelines for hand quilters, upon which most quilters will agree.

Lines marked for hand quilting must be totally removable after quilting. Choose marking tools that will produce clear, easy-to-see, fine lines that do not alter the appearance of the fabric after they are removed. The marker should leave lines that are easy to see, but do not damage the quilt with residue or by the pressure required to mark the quilt.

It's likely that you will need several different types of markers for use on light and dark fabrics. Most dry and wet markers come in a variety of colors. You will need to experiment to find the most useful kinds of markers for the kinds of designs you like to quilt and for your eyesight.

Always use a very light touch when marking, and mark only the critical parts of the design.

Dry Markers

• **Chalk** - Sharpened, common blackboard chalk is a good marker for dark fabrics. Do not use chalks made for artists. Large quilts may need to be remarked. It is very easy to remove by brushing.

• **Powdered chalk with applicator** - It is easy to use, but large quilts may need to be remarked. It is moderately easy to remove by brushing or with art gum eraser or non-detergent soap and water.

• **Graphite pencils** - Hard drawing pencils can be used. Keep them sharp and use a very light touch. Do not use soft, common, #2 pencils because they will make your thread and quilt top dirty. Remove with art gum eraser or non-detergent soap and water.

• **Dressmaker pencils** - These are not recommended as they can be very difficult to remove.

• **Dressmaker chalk** - Good on dark and light fabrics and for marking small areas. Remove by brushing or with art gum eraser or non-detergent soap and water.

• **Soap slivers** - These leftovers from the bathroom are good for marking small areas on dark fabrics. Use non-oily soap slivers only. Remove with water or by brushing.

• **Silver pencils** - They are good for marking large areas on dark and light fabrics. Remove with art gum eraser or non-detergent soap and water.

• **Yellow pencils** - They are good for marking large areas on dark and light fabrics. Use with caution as they are often difficult to remove. Remove with art gum eraser or non-detergent soap and water.

• **White pencils** - They are good for marking large areas on dark fabric. Remove with art gum eraser or non-detergent soap and water.

• **Soapstone** - This is a hard mineral that is good for marking small areas on dark fabric. Use a broken edge or sharpen it with a pencil sharpener. Remove with water or by brushing.

Water Soluble Markers

• **Pencils** - Use like graphite pencils or chalk. They are good for marking large areas. Remove with water.

• **Fiber-tip markers** - They are good for marking large areas. Remove with water.

Timely Tip: It is best to remove water soluble markings with a power-jet hose attached to the faucet. Simply dabbing with water is likely to leave a residue by forcing the marking liquid to the back of the quilt and not out of the quilt. Force the marking compound through and out of the quilt with a strong jet of water.

Disappearing Markers

• **Fiber-tip markers** - They are good for marking small areas. Lines disappear in a short time.

• **Stylus or blunt darning needle** - Marks are made by indented pressure lines on the fabric. It is good for small areas to be quilted in a short period of time since lines are self removing.

Other Supplies

• **Manual pencil sharpener** - Hand sharpening your marking pencils is more economical than using an electric sharpener.

• **1/4" masking tape** - This is used for creating an accurate distance from seam lines. Teachers call this tape, "Training wheels for hand quilters!" Remove tape as soon as possible as it can leave a residue on the quilt.

• **1/2" and 1" masking tape** - This is used for making quick background quilting line grids. Remove tape as soon as possible as it can leave a residue on the quilt.

Timely Tips
• Some markers, even those made for quilting, can leave permanent marks on fabric. Some markers are "set" by heat, sunlight, or laundry detergents. Do not iron any fabric that has been marked.

• Test all markers on all fabrics used in a quilt. Test for visibility and removeability.

• Remove all marking lines. Working lines left on the quilt are unsightly distractions from the beauty of your work.

• Try marking and quilting a very dark quilt from the back side of the quilt.

Frames and Hoops

The quality of your hand-quilting stitch will improve with the use of a hoop or frame. Hoops and frames stretch and hold the quilt allowing the hands freedom to quilt. They are manufactured in wood and in plastic. They come in sizes suitable for one quilter, or many quilters, to work on a quilt.

Quilting frames and hoops are made of heavier materials than are frames and hoops designed for embroidery or needlepoint. They are made to accommodate the three layers of the quilt and they need to be sturdy and smooth. A well-made frame or hoop should last you a lifetime.

Lap Hoops and Frames

Good hand-quilting technique does not require a large frame. Wonderful quilts are hand quilted on laps! However, one would be wrong to think that no frame or hoop is used when reading about "lap quilting." There are many kinds of lap-size frames and hoops available to modern day hand-quilters.

Smaller frames and hoops should be supported by a table while you are seated in a chair or by drawn-up knees if you are seated on a couch.

WOODEN HOOPS

Wooden hoops come in many sizes, both in round and oval shapes. There are varieties that use a top hoop and screw to tighten the quilt into the bottom hoop as well as styles that use a large elastic band over the lower hoops for stretching the quilt. Specialty half-hoops are made for hand quilting borders. Wooden hoops are practically indestructible if kept dry. A section of a quilt is worked on while the remainder lies on the lap or is draped over a table.

If you are limited in space and have never used a hand-quilting frame, I suggest you buy a wooden 14" or 16" circle hoop. The wood should be smooth without splinters or dings. You will probably have this hoop for the rest of your life—buy the best quality you can afford.

PLASTIC FRAMES

Plastic frames come in several rectangular and square sizes. The plastic rail frames have half-circle bars that snap over the rails clamping the quilt tightly. These frames are easy to assemble. Plastic frame parts can warp in the presence of extreme heat. A section of a quilt is worked on while the remainder lies on the lap or is draped over a table.

WOODEN RAIL FRAMES

Four wooden rails, usually 18" to 24" in length, are held together with bolts and wing-nuts. These stretcher bars have cloth stapled to the sides. They are adjustable in size. A section of the quilt is pinned to the cloth and the frame is stretched out and secured tightly with bolts and wing-nuts. A section of a quilt is worked on while the remainder lies on the lap or is draped over a table.

Timely Tip: My lap-quilting projects are kept clean and ready to quilt in plastic bags. I've transported my smaller hand-quilting projects around the world in these bags. The large white bags with drawstrings are better looking and less objectionable than the super-sized brown or black variety. Of course, finished quilts are not stored in plastic bags.

Free-standing Frames

WOODEN RAIL FRAMES

Free-standing rail frames are practical when you will be able to finish a quilt without having to remove it from the frame before it is finished. This assumes that you will do all your hand quilting, seated with the frame, while located in one spot where you can leave it up for a long period of time. There are many kinds of rail frames available.

Four-Square frames are made by using four long rails made from 2" x 2" or 2" x 4" lengths of cured lumber and "C" clamps. Strips of striped fabric are stapled along the length of each rail. The four rails rest on the backs of chairs or saw horses. Quilt is layered and basted into the frame. Quilting begins at the edges of the frame and is worked toward the middle.

Rail and Ratchet frames are fitted with horizontal rails and ratchets (cogs) that allow the quilter to control the tension of the quilt layers. Frames can have two to four rails depending on the way the quilt is attached to the frame and the sophistication of the system.

PLASTIC FRAMES

Free-standing plastic frames are a hybrid frame with plastic pieces that clamp over plastic rails like a hoop. The quilter works at a section of the quilt while seated in a chair at the frame. These frames require little floor space. It is easy to put a quilt into the frame and to remove it for storage. They are very portable. I've made a patchwork bag for my plastic floor frame and carry it with me for quilting stitch demonstrations.

HOOPS ON STANDS AND PEDESTALS

A **large oval or circular hoop on a free-standing stand or pedestal** can be a good compromise between the very large rail quilting frames and a hoop or frame held in the lap. They are smaller, portable, and are often made like fine pieces of furniture. The small standing frame supports the weight of the quilt while the quilter is seated in a chair or on a couch.

Needles

Quilters use a family of hand-quilting needles called betweens. Folklore, possibly based in truth, says that these needles come by their name because they are designed with attributes somewhere between sharps and darning needles.

Betweens come in different sizes. A #7 is the largest between needle that's readily available. A #12 needle is the smallest size. The needle sizes, like women's shoes, vary between brands. Experienced quilters keep a good supply of their favorite size and brand. I alternately use #10 and #12 needles—as my use depends on the fabric, the batting, my mood and, I suspect, the position of the stars and the moon.

Besides strength, the second most important attribute of the needle is the specific definition between the shaft of the needle and the point, **Fig 1**. The experienced hand quilter can feel the needle hesitate when the whole point, alone, has penetrated the quilt layers. That is the precise moment that the needle must be turned back up through from the bottom layer.

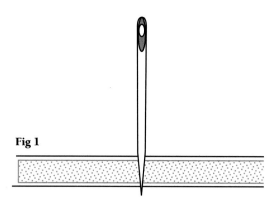

Fig 1

> *Timely Tips*
> • *The drop of the needle point through the three layers, determines the length of the stitch on the back of the quilt!*
> • *The smaller between needles are sometimes difficult to pull through the layers of the quilt—especially when you've placed several stitches on the needle. To make it easier to grip that pesky needle, use a rubber finger pad, from a stationary store, on the index finger. Wear the rubber pad while you are becoming accustomed to the thimble.*
> • *Do not use bent needles.*

A SHARP DECISION

Sharp needles are very good for piecing patchwork and embroidery, but they are not designed for fine hand quilting. A sharp needle is designed with a very long and sharp point that starts just below the eye of the needle. A sharp needle glides through the fabric or quilt layers too easily, making it difficult to determine how much of the needle is through the fabric.

Thimbles

A thimble is a necessary tool for hand quilters. It doesn't matter what kind of thimble you use as long as it has deep dimples (indentations) on the sides and the end. The indentations are used to hold the eye end of the needle in order to guide it through the quilt layers.

The thimble is used to protect the middle finger of the top quilting hand. Useful thimbles are made from metals, plastic, hard rubber, and leather with metal inserts. They come in cap shapes, open-ended, and partially-opened for longer fingernails. They come in various sizes so don't buy a thimble unless you can try it on.

Fitting Your Thimble

The thimble should fit the tip of the middle finger to the first joint. It should fit firmly without undue pressure on the knuckle. A good test for fit is to put the thimble on your finger, spread your fingers and shake your hand fairly vigorously. A well-fitting thimble won't turn on your finger or drop off.

I strongly suggest buying and trying several inexpensive thimbles. Don't develop too special a kinship with only one thimble. Thimbles get lost, stepped on, chewed by the dog and get holes in them. The cost of a thimble, in my experience, has little to with value.

With experience, you may want to buy a few very sturdy thimbles with extra features that may help your stitch improve—you are only human. However, remember that a NEW-AND-IMPROVED thimble does not contain magic. Only practice with a well-fitting deep-dimpled thimble will improve the quality of your hand-quilting stitch.

> *Timely Tips*
> • *When you find thimbles that meet your hand-quilting criteria, buy several—include buying one at least a size smaller and one a size larger than you normally use. There will be times when your finger tip will be smaller or larger than normal. Be prepared!*
> • *Bathe your thimbles with alcohol now and then. Keep them clean and dry to prevent rust on the thimble or a fungus on your finger nail.*

Protecting the Under Hand

I don't recommend the use of thimbles on the under hand. The fingers on the lower hand need to feel the needle as it is passed from the top to the underside. As your quilting technique improves, you'll be able to control the pressure of the needle and feel it very quickly on the sensitive fingers on the underside of the quilt. Don't be afraid of the needle. Learning to hand quilt is a lot less painful than learning to ride a bicycle—remember all those scraped knees?

If protection is needed after prolonged quilting or after a major miscalculation resulting in a puncture, apply a product called New-Skin® Antiseptic Liquid Bandage which provides a light protective layer.

Thread

Choose strong, firm quilting threads of either 100% cotton or cotton-covered polyester. The thread must not easily break or fray at the ends. Softer, speciality threads can be used for hand-quilted projects that are not expected to see much use or wear.

Hand quilting threads come in a wide range of colors. Use any color you find that enhances your quilt. More than one color thread on a quilt is acceptable as long as the results are appropriate and are not distracting.

A beginning hand quilter will find matching the thread color to the predominant fabric color will hide uneven or larger quilting stitches. More advanced hand quilters will want to show off their small even stitches by using contrasting thread. When teaching, I ask my beginning and intermediate hand quilters to use contrasting thread. This results in a fair evaluation of their progress.

Thread does age and deteriorate. Keep it away from excessive light, heat, soiling and moisture. Don't stockpile thread. Buy all your thread as needed from stores and shops that keep fresh supplies. Keep your grandmother's quilting thread as a memento. Don't use it in your quilts.

I don't recommend the use of beeswax for coating quilting thread as it attracts soil and causes the thread to drag through the batting. Often it causes the batting to stick to the thread, aggravating fiber migration.

> *Timely Tips*
> • *Make threading easier by cutting the end of the thread at an angle.*
> • *Thread all your needles onto the spool of thread at one time,* **Fig 2**—*use as needed!*

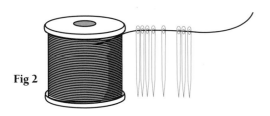

Fig 2

Quilting Stencils

Quilting stencils and patterns sometimes look peculiar to beginning hand quilters. They usually come with little or no instruction as to how to get the design from the stencil or paper onto the quilt top.

Stencils are made commercially from plastic and cardboard. They come in many styles and patterns. Stencils often have bridges connecting parts of the design, **Fig 3**. These areas are not part of the design. They are just there to keep the stencil from falling apart!

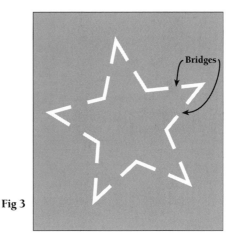

Fig 3

Stencils can be positive space designs where the design is cut out along the outer edge, **Fig 4A** or negative space designs where the design is cut out of a larger shape, **Fig 4B**.

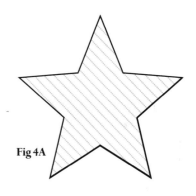

Fig 4A

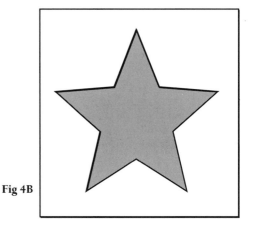

Fig 4B

A simple motif can be overlapped, **Fig 5A** or repeated to create many complex and interesting quilting patterns, **Fig 5B**.

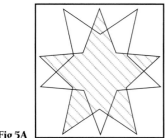

Fig 5A

Fig 5B

Making Stencils

Copy the quilting pattern onto plain paper or freezer paper. Be accurate. Glue the plain paper copy onto an old manila file folder. If you use freezer paper you can iron the copy to the file folder. Then, cut out the template with paper scissors or a craft knife.

Super Tip for Computer Users: I scan my own quilting pattern drawings into the computer and print them out onto freezer paper that has been hand-trimmed to fit the printer.

Quilting Patterns

The choice of a quilting pattern can make or break the overall effect of a quilted project. Even though each new piece to be quilted will require special consideration, there are a few guidelines to aid you in the choice of patterns.

Plainly stated, plain quilts usually need fancier quilting than busy or intricate quilts. However a quilt is quilted, the patterns should be appropriate to the style and use of the project. As my son Stephen once said, "I don't want any butterflies or flowers on my quilt." He was a manly four year old at the time.

Good quilting patterns are planned as integral parts of the total design. The patterns should enhance the overall effect of the finished quilt giving it added detail and richness. Quilting designs that look lively at a distance and still offer sufficient interest close-up are most effective.

The following drawings, **Figs 6A** to **6C**, used with permission from the archives of The Stearns Technical Textiles Company, illustrate three quilt designs that include specific hand-quilting patterns coordinated for each quilt. Patterns for these quilts are still available from the company.

Some quilts, for example the Double Wedding Bands (**A**), have large open areas that demand interesting and varied quilting patterns, while in other quilts the principle design fills the quilt, making elaborate quilting patterns redundant, as in the Twinkling Star (**B**). In the Dew Drop Quilt (**C**), we see a perfect blending of appliqué technique with elaborate hand-quilting patterns.

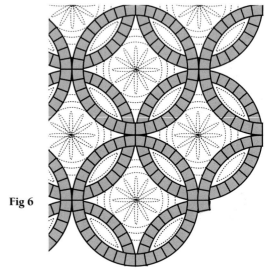

Fig 6

A - Double Wedding Bands

B - Twinkling Star

C - Dew Drop

At no time should large open areas be left in hand-quilted projects. A good and simple test for the maximum area that may be left non-quilted is to place a closed fist onto the quilt. It should touch quilting on each side of the fist, **Fig 7**.

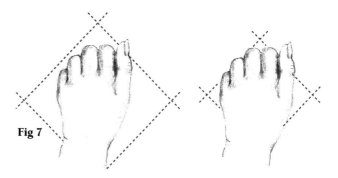

Fig 7

When quilting a grid of several lines on a large quilt, it is best to work in a zigzag manner rather than in long straight lines, **Fig 8**. A long line of quilting can become stressed and snap if the quilt is pulled in that direction. A zigzag line of quilting acts like a spring snapping back into position.

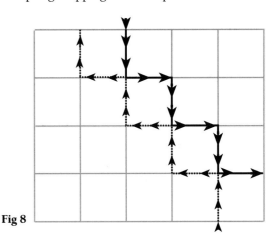

Fig 8

Traditional and modern quilting stitch patterns and templates are widely available to the hand quilter. Books and other publications are found in quilt, fabric and craft shops offering hundreds of designs in coordinated groups for blocks, corners and various width borders. Coordination is the key in choosing quilting stitch patterns. A select variety of coordinated patterns will add value to a project while an indifferent selection, just for novelty sake, will look hodgepodge.

As in all aspects of quilting, the patterns chosen for the quilting stitch will reflect the needs and personality of the quilter with the following cautions:

When planning the quilting patterns, the quilter must remember to use patterns that meet the minimum requirements of the batting used. This information should be listed on the bag or offered on a product information sheet. See the Batting Chart, page 5.

Hand Quilting Patchwork

Quilting one quarter inch away from the seam edges or in-the-ditch (at the seam) are most often the techniques used for over-all patchwork quilts, **Fig 9**.

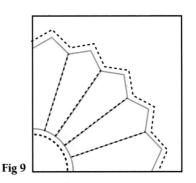

Fig 9

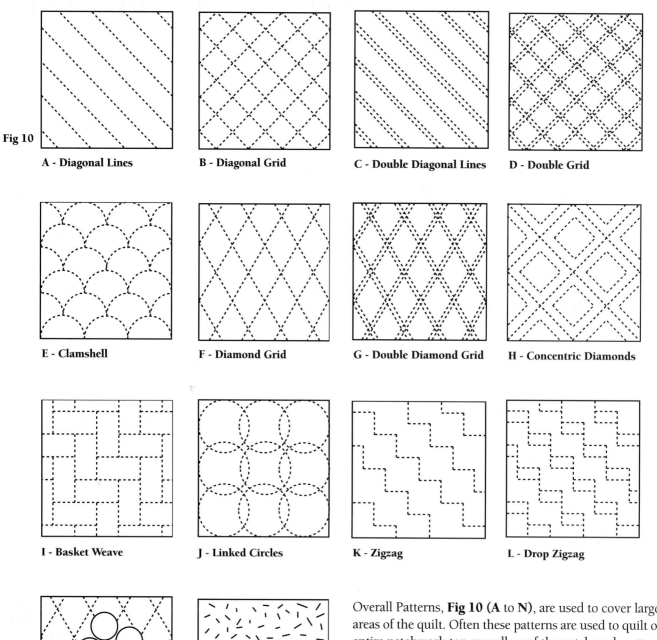

Fig 10

A - Diagonal Lines

B - Diagonal Grid

C - Double Diagonal Lines

D - Double Grid

E - Clamshell

F - Diamond Grid

G - Double Diamond Grid

H - Concentric Diamonds

I - Basket Weave

J - Linked Circles

K - Zigzag

L - Drop Zigzag

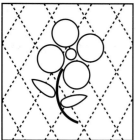

M - Diamond Grid around Single Motif

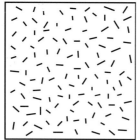

N - Stipple Quilting

Overall Patterns, **Fig 10 (A** to **N)**, are used to cover large open areas of the quilt. Often these patterns are used to quilt over an entire patchwork top regardless of the patchwork pattern.

Border and Corner Patterns are used to frame the whole quilt or portions of the quilt. There are several sub-categories for these patterns: cables; feathers; vines; geometrics; and garlands. The Amish Style Quilt, page 26, and the Pumpkin Seed Quilt, page 23, illustrate borders, corner turns, and single motifs.

Single Motif Patterns are used as focal points in a quilt. They can be used single or in groups and in combination with border and background patterns. All of the quilts in this book feature one or more single motif patterns.

GETTING READY TO HAND QUILT

Marathon runners train for the long endurance run. I like to think of hand quilters as marathoners who deserve a ribbon at the finish line each and every time we finish a hand-quilted quilt!

If you are seated in an uncomfortable position with poor lighting, you won't enjoy the process for very long. Hand quilting under bad conditions is like running a marathon in poor shoes - ouch! Here are some suggestions for your comfort and enjoyment of hand quilting.

Posture

Your endurance and enjoyment of hand quilting can depend on your posture while sitting with a lap hoop or at a free-standing frame. Try using a foot stool under your feet and try placing a small pillow at the hollow of the back for added support.

Try keeping your shoulders back and your spine straight. Find your optimum height (the distance from the quilt to your eyes) for hand quilting and adjust the frame or your chair to that position. If you are working with a group, carry your own chair, lighting or booster seat—whatever will make you comfortable.

Change body position often to relax your small and larger muscles. Do stretching exercises for your hands, arms and large muscles every thirty minutes or so.

Lighting

Good even lighting is essential for hand quilting. Normal home lighting can be augmented with draftsmen's lights that can be attached to tables or inexpensive clip-on lights from a discount store. When I lap quilt at home, I favor my light-filled breakfast room and I travel with a clip-on light.

Timely Tips
- *For the left-handed quilter, the strongest light should come over the right shoulder.*
- *For the right-handed quilter, the strongest light should come over the left shoulder.*
- *You will need twice your normal light requirement to work on a dark quilt.*

Breathing

Breathing is a good thing. Many beginning quilters hold their breath between hand quilting stitches. Don't do that—relax and breathe normally. The time you spend hand quilting should be a relaxing, gentle, rather repetitive activity that will allow your mind to wander.

Mental Attitude

Develop the right mental attitude about hand quilting. You are making something enduring in a grand tradition. Do it because you enjoy the process and the results. Hand quilters must learn to look at their work with a long view perspective. The beauty of the technique is that it really can't be hurried and some days it cannot be done well at all.

There will be days when you probably should not be quilting. Go ahead and rake the leaves, clean the bath tub, take a ride on your bike; do anything other than quilting. If you try to force yourself to hand quilt when your body and mind are telling you "NO…not today, thank you…" you will end up ripping it out or wishing you had.

The Physical World

Your physical surroundings and physical state can also affect your ability to hand quilt and the quality of your work. If you wake up one morning and don't feel as spunky or as energetic as you normally do, the quality of your work will be affected. Modify your expectations for the day. That's all right.

I know from personal experience that the quality of my hand quilting is quite poor when I work in a humid climate and use a cotton batting. I live and normally work in a very dry climate. If I modify my expectations, use a thinner between needle, and rub the needle through my hair, I can come close to my normal stitch.

Timely Tip: As a child, I thought it was funny when my Grandma ran the point of her needle through her shiny black hair. Now I know she was coating the tip of the needle with a little oil for lubrication! It works.

As you age or physically change, you may want to modify your expectations regarding your hand-quilting stitch. You are not lowering your standards. You are reacting, positively and realistically, to physical changes. As Winston Churchill said, "Never, never, never, never give up."

A perfect hand quilting technique, which results in perfect, even, small, stitches, is an exquisite thing. There is, possibly, an equal beauty in the halting stitches of a novice quilter and the less than straight oversized stitches of a senior hand. The common thread is a love of the work and the hand-quilting tradition.

HAND QUILTING

Hand quilting can be one of the most enjoyable and relaxing of all needlework. You are thinking—"Right, easy for her to say." Let me tell you some things you need to know about hand quilting.

You must relax and open up your hands. Do not try to quilt with either of your hands in a tight little ball. When you draw your fingers into the palm of your hand, you are "stressing out" the small muscles and nerves all the way up to your elbow. Some people "fist up" so tightly that the pull is felt all the way up into the shoulders. Try it—make a fist. Can you feel the pull? You won't be able to quilt for long periods of time if your hand, arm and shoulders hurt and ache. We won't even discuss the long term results of this constant stress on your muscles and nerves.

No-Stress Hand Quilting

The secret to stress-free hand quilting is to keep your hand open while quilting. Try it—your hand is not under stress when you open and spread the fingers slightly. This is the technique I use, having learned it from my grandmother and our relatives. I can hand quilt until my mind turns to mush, my underhand is numb, and I have to be helped to a standing position, but my top hand is still relaxed, painless and stress free.

Preparing the Fabric for Hand Quilting

Beginning hand quilters should use, topweight, 100% cotton fabrics. Use solid or printed fabrics with an even weave. Do not use broadcloths for hand quilting as they are not of an even weave.

Pre-wash all fabric to be used in hand quilting. Iron the fabric. Stretch at the corners of the fabric to align the grainline.

Tearing the fabric for borders and for the large squares used in a quilt top to be hand quilted is preferable to cutting with scissors or a rotary tool. It assures that the pieces are on the grain line. Accurate grain line is helpful when marking the fabric and when hand quilting.

If using patterned fabric pieces, they must be cut along the pattern of the fabric, regardless of the grain line. Extra care must be taken when measuring fabric that is cut and not torn.

A quilting design can be aligned, correctly, with the grain line in preparation for marking and the marking is more precise when the fabric grain line is true. Accurate grain line is critical when marking background grids for hand quilting.

Borders and squares are more accurately assembled with little or no warping of the pieces if the grain line is true.

Hand quilting is easier if the grain line is consistent throughout the piece. The quilter is better able to anticipate areas where the hand stitch might need to be modified. Grain line is less critical for a patchwork block or for an all over patchwork quilt than it is for an appliqué or another quilt with large areas of a single fabric.

Marking the Quilt

To mark your quilt using a stencil, place stencil where you want the design on the quilt top; mark through the open areas. *Note: When quilting, quilt through unmarked bridge areas as well as marked areas.*

To mark your quilt using a quilt design from a book or pattern, trace design onto tracing paper. Pin traced design to underside of quilt top where desired. Tape fabric up to a sunny window and trace pattern as the light shows through the paper and fabric. A light box is a good tool for tracing designs.

Layering the Quilt

When your quilt top is finished, press flat.

For quilt backing, cut or tear the fabric to a measurement of four inches larger than the top of the quilt. Tape the backing fabric wrong side up to a table top. Stretch it out firmly, but not excessively taut.

Trim batting one to two inches larger than quilt top. Layer batting over backing.

Place quilt top centered on batting with the right side up.

Using a long, sharp needle and a light-colored thread, baste the three layers together beginning in the center of the quilt and working toward the edges.

Putting the Quilt into a Hoop or Small Frame

Find a hoop or frame to fit your project. If your hoop fits the quilt top—roll edges of backing over edge of quilt top a quarter of an inch and baste down.

If your hoop is larger than the quilt top, extend the top by basting scrap strips through all three layers, **Fig 1**. Work from the top of the quilt.

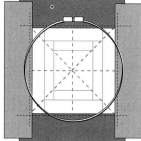

Fig 1

Place quilt sandwich in the hoop, allowing for some slack. The quilt should appear somewhat relaxed in the frame. It shouldn't be stretched taut or "at attention."

> *Timely Tip:* To prepare a quilt for hand quilting, stretch the quilt firmly in the hoop (or frame). Check the top and bottom for smoothness (no puckers or wrinkles). Next, gently rub the heel of your hand across the top surface to relax the tension. My Grandma said, "...it should look as if a cat slept on it." In our house that look is easily achieved as the cats line up awaiting their turn on the newest quilt—turning it into an impromptu sleeping hammock.

Putting the Quilt into a Large Frame

Put the layered quilt onto the frame. Each style of floor frame will have different instructions for attaching the layered quilt to the frame.

Note: When there is too great a difference in size between the quilt and the quilting frame, baste strips to the sides of the quilt.

> *Timely Tip:* When quilting elaborate quilts, stitch all straight line quilting on a large free standing frame; then, take the quilt off the large frame and complete the more detailed work, in a lap hoop.

Now, It's Time to Quilt

To Knot or Not to Knot?

That is a serious question. I'm a confirmed knotter and I'll tell you why. Grandma Ritzenthalar did not often put knots in her quilts and parts of her quilts are coming apart. I could spend every evening of my life mending unknotted seams and quilting that has come undone with common use. Make and use discrete knots for piecing, appliqué and hand quilting, unless you want your grandchildren to do a lot of mending.

Knots in Patchwork

Working from the top of the quilt, hide the knot in the seam allowance of the darkest fabric. Poke the knot in through the darkest fabric and out from the darkest fabric. If the fabric is of a loose weave, make a second knot about 1/4" from quilt top; insert it in the same hole that the thread is coming out, and come back up in opposite direction from first knot.

Knots in Open Areas

Working from the top, put needle into the quilt under the line to be quilted. The needle will be going in the opposite direction that you will be quilting, **Fig 2**. Bring needle back to surface and gently pop the knot into the quilt and batting by giving a short, quick tug. Quilting will begin over the imbedded knot

and tail of the quilting thread. The quilting covers the shadow of the knot and tail of the thread, **Fig 3**.

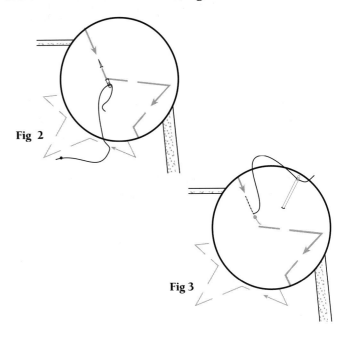

Fig 2

Fig 3

Reminder: Don't imbed the knot by coming in from the side of the line to be quilted as the shadow of the thread might show on the surface of the quilt.

The Dimple Style Stitch for Stress-free Hand Quilting

For the Dimple Style Stitch, the needle is pushed through the layers (backing, batting and top) in a vertical position, by the side of the thimble, using an exaggerated rocking and rolling motion of the two hands. An attempt is made to keep the needle in as vertical a position as possible throughout the completion of each stitch. This vertical positioning creates the signature "dimple." The thimble finger controls the stitch from start to finish. The thumb and forefinger pull the needle through after each run of stitches.

Step 1. To begin, set the point of the needle into the quilt in a true vertical position, **Fig 4**. Hold the needle in place with the side of the thimble on top. The point of the needle rests on the middle finger underneath. The pressure of a finger on the underside of the quilt helps to hold it vertical.

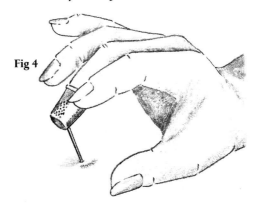

Fig 4

The eye of the needle rests on the side of the thimble at all times.

Step 2. Hold the point of the needle on the under finger as you push that finger up and roll it toward the top thumb. With the top thumb, press down on the quilt toward the thimble, **Figs 5a and 5b**.

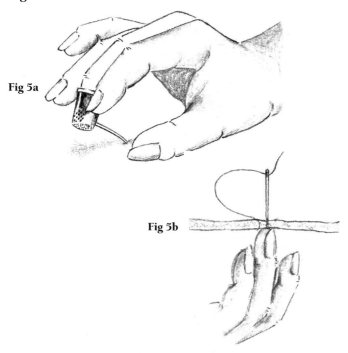

Fig 5a

Fig 5b

At the same time, rock the needle shaft horizontal to the quilt. Press your thumb down to trap the quilt between the under finger and the thumb, with the needle in between. The point will have come through to just touch your top thumb, **Figs 6a and 6b**.

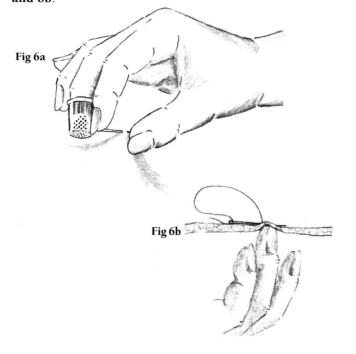

Fig 6a

Fig 6b

Note: This pressure will arc the needle a little. As soon as you see the point and it touches or almost touches your thumb, move the needle back to an exaggerated vertical position.

Step 3. It is all right if you can only take one stitch at a time. As you gain experience and hand-eye control, you'll be able to make a stitching run of several stitches of the same length.

If you are finishing only one stitch, it is time to push the needle all the way through, pull the needle out and get ready for the next run of stitches.

If you feel you can continue with this run of stitches go on to Step 4 and 5 without stopping.

Step 4. Repeat Step 1. With the needle in the vertical position push point ONLY through to the underside finger, **Fig 7**. Only the point of the needle is felt by the under finger—never the shaft of the needle. If you see or feel the shaft of the needle your stitch will be long.

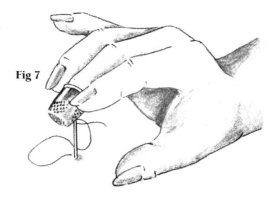

Fig 7

Step 5. Repeat Step 2. Hold the point of the needle on the under finger as you push that finger up and roll it toward the top thumb, **Fig 8**.

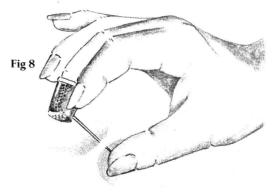

Fig 8

With the top thumb, press down on the quilt toward the thimble. At the same time, rock the needle shaft horizontal to the quilt. Press your thumb down to trap the quilt between the under finger and the thumb, with the needle in between a pincer-like motion. The point will have come through to just touch your top thumb.

Note: It will be harder to push the needle to the exaggerated vertical position as you place more and more stitches on the needle. Smaller *stitches make it easier to put the needle in the vertical position each time. Each time you re-position the needle to the vertical position, you will see a dimple form on the quilt, **Fig 9**.*

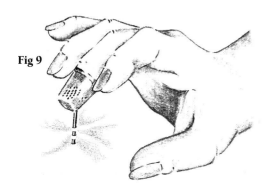

Fig 9

Rock the needle horizontal to the quilt and push only the point of the needle through the top of the quilt. The point touches or almost touches your thumb.

Step 6. Repeat Step 1. More stitches are on the needle. The moment you see the point of the needle touch your thumb on the top of the quilt you rock the needle to the vertical position and push the point through to the backside touching the under finger.

I call this "two-point" acupuncture!

Step 7. If you've reached your limit of stitches, **Fig 10**, push the needle through the last stitch and finish the run. Begin again at Step 1.

Fig 10

Step 8. For you over-achievers! Notice how the needle is in an exaggerated vertical position with four or five stitches on the needle, **Fig 11**. To keep the quality of stitches the same on top and back, one must slightly alter the position of the hands and needle as the run of stitches carry more and more stitches on the needle.

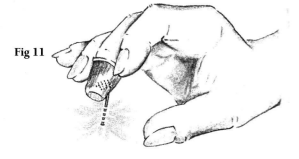

Fig 11

Ending the Thread

Make a double knot in the quilting thread about one quarter of an inch above the quilt; put the needle directly back into the place it last came out of the quilt, **Fig 12**.

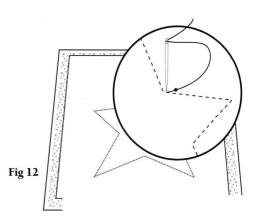

Fig 12

Push the needle deep into the batting under the finished quilting line (but not through to the backing). Bring the needle to the surface at the beginning or end of an existing stitch and give a gentle tug (knot will be buried in batting), **Fig 13** .Cut thread close to surface of quilt. If the fabric is of a loose weave or you are uncertain about your knot repeat the process again, reversing the needle. The under shadow of quilting thread should always be under a quilting line, not out to the side. This technique for stopping eliminates most gaps on the back of the quilt.

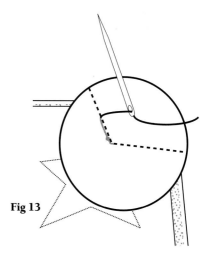

Fig 13

17

HOW TO IMPROVE YOUR QUILTING STITCH

The art of hand quilting endures because nothing can duplicate the look of fine hand quilting. Hand quilting takes time and practice, and more time and more practice.

Try following some of these Timely tips for improving your quilting stitch. They are answers to questions posed to me by students over the seventeen years I've taught the class called Grandma's Quilting Stitch:

What is the biggest mistake you see in hand quilting? Using too thick a batting. Use a low-loft, thin batting. If you want a fluffy comforter-type quilt, tie it. Look at old hand-quilted quilts. There is not much loft in them—they are flat. Split the batting if the type you bought has too much loft and is hard to quilt. Sometimes it is still too thick and you will need to split it again!

What kind of batting do you use? For larger quilts, I will use a polyester batting with a loft that will show off my hand quilting. I'm much more adventuresome with smaller quilts. I'll use any lower loft batting or any fiber. I do record, on the quilt label, what kind of batting is used in each of my hand-quilted quilts.

What do you mean when you say my stitch is irregular? Look at **Fig 1** below. The one on the left looks like someone is sending Morse Code—the stitches are irregular. The sample on the right is more regular. Practice the same simple design over and over until you can control your stitches.

Fig 1

My first stitches of the day are really bad. Is there help? Exercise your hands before beginning on your project. Even after you have started to hand quilt a full-size bed quilt, it is a good idea to keep a small project going. Use it to warm up and keep the small muscles at-the-ready by working a few minutes every day on a small project.

I don't like starting or ending a run of quilting. Help? Plan your quilting path before you begin. Where can a run of quilting go? Look at the Pumpkin Seed Quilt, **Fig 1** on page 21. Try for the longest run you can make with a single eighteen inch thread!

Do I need to move the frame if I want to continue quilting along a line? I hate to knot and end the thread there. Don't move the frame or knot the thread. Continue the last bit of the run close to the edge of the frame, and leave the needle in the quilt until you can complete the run after you've moved the frame. I will sometimes have eight or ten needles in the quilt and at-the-ready for when I've moved the frame.

How many stitches to the inch should I make? Make as many as you can as long as they are even and appear the same on the top and back of your quilt. Beginners might be happy with five stitches to the inch. Intermediate quilters might make nine or ten stitches to the inch. Advanced hand quilters will strive for twelve to sixteen in that space.

I've heard that quilt judges count the stitches. Is that true? I can't say it is never done, but I've never counted quilting stitches when judging, and I've never seen a judge count stitches. Experienced judges KNOW a good quilting stitch when they see it.

How do I perfect my quilting stitch? I'll let you know when I find something better than practice. I've been hand quilting most of my life and I'll let you in on a secret. I have an excellent stitch, under the right circumstances, about twenty-five percent of the time. I have a good stitch about fifty percent of the time and twenty-five percent of the time, I shouldn't have a needle in my hand! Hand quilting is about hand and hand-eye control. Practice setting the needle through the quilt layers and resting it on the under finger. Practice pushing the needle straight up and down in one place without taking a stitch. Force your hands to trust each other.

My first stitch is awful! Help? The easiest stitch to control should be your first stitch. It does, however, seem to cause the most trouble. Because you are setting the needle in place for the run of stitches, you must place it equidistant from the last stitch. You judge that distance with your eyes.

I have trouble keeping the needle on the thimble. What am I doing wrong? Get a thimble with deeper dimples. Try a soft rubber or soft plastic thimble.

My thimble turns on my finger as I quilt. What's wrong? You need a smaller thimble.

Help! My quilting thread shows through the top when I've passed through from one area to another! When you pass through, or travel, you need to slip your needle deep under the batting. Don't let the needle and thread skim just under the top layer.

I've never worn a thimble before. Will it always feel like a club on my hand? A well-fitting thimble will become like a natural part of your hand if you will just WEAR IT. Wear it to the grocery store. Wear it while you car pool. It will become so much a part of you that you will find yourself in strange places with your thimble on. I've discovered mine on my hand at weddings, in church, on airplanes, on a doctor's examination table.

What's wrong with my stitches? They are not the same on the back as the front. First check the quality of the fabric on the back of the quilt. Does it have the same thread count? Is it the same weight fabric? Next, check your technique. The amount of needle beyond the point that you allow to drop through the back of the quilt, determines the length of that backstitch. The amount of needle that comes through the top, before you turn the needle vertical again, determines the length of the top stitch. These should be of equal length to produce a consistent stitch top and back.

Does fabric grain line affect my hand quilting? YES! It's easier to quilt on the diagonal (bias) of a fabric. It is harder to quilt with the grain line. That's why experienced quilters love quilting diagonal grids. You can't always avoid quilting on the grain line, of course, but you can learn to modify your technique so that it doesn't feel as if you've hit a brick wall when you change directions.

What about seam allowances? How do I quilt through them? Don't if at all possible. Pass through most patchwork seam allowances, **Fig 2**.

When I start and stop a line of quilting, I leave a gap on the back of the quilt. What do I need to do? As your stitches get smaller, the gap will not be as noticeable or may disappear. Most quilters develop personal techniques for making compensating stitches as they start or finish. Don't get into the habit of backstitching to compensate, as that makes a really messy back of quilt.

My quilting thread keeps fraying and breaking! What am I doing wrong? There are at least two reasons for breaking thread. Start quilting with a single 18" length of thread knotted at one end. A longer thread will often wear out before you are ready to make your finishing knot. Remember to use new thread. Another reason thread frays or breaks is because there is a burr, a rough irregularity, in the eye of the needle. It might be cutting through the delicate fibers that make up your quilting thread. Change needles if this occurs.

I'm a lefty. Can left-handed people create the dimpled quilting stitch? Of course you can—with practice. The only difference is in the position of the hands—they face the opposite direction.

The quilt judge said my "…stitches need improvement." What did the judge mean? Ask yourself the following questions. Are the stitches even, the same size, on the top and bottom of the quilt? Are there traveling stitches on the back of the quilt where you've moved to another area? Do you have backstitches that show on the back or front of your quilt? Are your straight lines straight and your curved lines smooth? Are your stitches relatively small? If you've responded "no" to any of those questions you've found your answer.

Sometimes it's hard to read the comments from quilt judges. Try to think of the judging process as the next to last part of the quilting process, the evaluation. The final part of the process is improvement. Just think to yourself, "…I'll show them"!

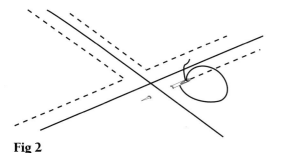

Fig 2

THE PRACTICE PIECES

It's easier and less intimidating if you start your practice on small projects that you can complete quickly (or not complete if you don't want to). The first two quilt designs in this section are each small enough to be completed in a relaxing evening or two. You may want to use one of these two designs to try out the techniques explained previously in this book. Once you are reasonably comfortable with your hand quilting stitch and feel more ambitious, you are ready to start in on the second two, more elaborate, designs. While you are practicing, relax and enjoy the process. Remember, the only way to improve your hand-quilting stitch is to practice.

LOVE TOKEN BUTTON QUILT

The center of this little quilt is a single paper-cut motif that you can use to practice and improve your quilting stitch. There are two rows of echo quilting around the single motif. Echo quilting repeats the contour of the central motif. This little quilt is embellished with several favorite antique shell buttons. It could be a special gift for a friend. . . . . page 21

PUMPKIN SEED QUILT

This small quilt pattern is a simple unified grouping of a single motif, a border with a corner turn and a background grid. The central motif and the border are made of a traditional hand quilting pattern called Pumpkin Seed. . . . . page 23

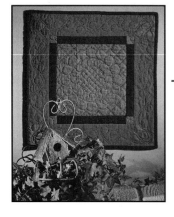

AMISH STYLE QUILT

A small feathered motif is in the center of this striking quilt. It features a single 1/2-inch grid in the center of the feathers, a double grid behind the feather and an open feather design in the second border. Quilting this lovely design will showcase your quilting stitches. . . . . page 26

WELCOME QUILT WITH WHEAT AND PINEAPPLE

This quilt is the most ambitious project of the book. It offers the opportunity of many relaxing hours of hand quilting. The pineapple and wheat symbols have been American signs of hospitality and welcome for centuries. The pineapple motif is an old butter mold design given to the author thirty years ago by Mary Cook Daniel, her mother-in-law. . . . . page 30

LOVE TOKEN BUTTON QUILT

Approximate Size: 12" x 12"
Center square: 6 1/2" x 6 1/2"

Materials & Supplies:

1/2 yd light-colored solid fabric for center and lining
1/8 yd print, first border
1/4 yd print, second border
1/2 yd each backing fabric and batting
freezer paper, 4 1/2" x 4 1/2" square
fabric marker
quilting thread, red and white
between quilting needle
small hoop

Quilting Pattern (page 22):

Snowflake Design

Cutting Requirements:

one 6 1/2" x 6 1/2" square, light-colored solid
one 16" x 16" square, light-colored solid
one 1 1/2" x 44" strip, first border fabric
one 4" x 44" strip, second border fabric
three 4" x 5" rectangles second border fabric for hanging tabs
16" x 16" square, backing fabric
16" x 16" square, batting

Instructions

Read pages 4 to 19 before beginning.

MAKING AN ORIGINAL PAPER QUILTING DESIGN
The quilting design used for the photographed model is included below, but a truly personal touch for any quilt is the use of paper-cut quilting stitch patterns. The easiest technique to use is the paper "snowflake" technique.

1. Fold 4 1/2" square of freezer paper in half and then in quarters. Make the folds crisp. Make one more fold on the diagonal to make a pad of paper in the shape of a triangle, **Fig 1**.

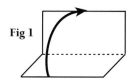

Fig 1

2. Sketch a design onto the folded triangle of paper, **Fig 2**. Cut the design out along drawn lines while the pad is still folded.

Fig 2

3. Open the folds to reveal the design, **Fig 3**.

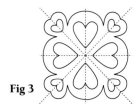

Fig 3

MAKING THE QUILT

1. Fold 6 1/2" fabric square in quarters. Gently finger press the folds. Do not stretch the fabric.

2. Center the paper-cut design over the folds, shiny side down; press in place with a warm iron.

3. After the fabric cools, use a fabric marker to transfer the design to the fabric by LIGHTLY drawing around the design. Pull up the freezer paper stencil and save it to use again on another quilt. Don't mark the echo quilting lines.

4. Sew borders to the center square along top and bottom edges first, then to sides.

Note: In order to protect the edge on the quilt, make the last border an inch or two larger than planned for the finished size. This excess is trimmed before binding.

5. Layer the 16" light-colored square, batting and quilt top; baste, then place in a hoop.

6. Begin quilting the Snowflake Design with red thread.

7. Echo quilt around outside edge of design with white thread one quarter of an inch away from Snowflake. Repeat with a second or third row of echo quilting.

8. Trim quilt to twelve inches square.

9. For hanging tabs, fold the 4" x 5" rectangles in half right sides together; stitch. Turn the tabs to the right side. Place one tab at the center of top edge of quilt with raw edges even; position remaining tabs in same manner about 3 1/4" from each side of center tab. Baste tabs in place.

10. Place 12" backing square right side down on quilt top; stitch along all four sides leaving an opening on one side for turning.

11. Turn quilt right side out through opening and blindstitch opening closed.

12. Fold tabs over and attach to the front of the quilt with buttons.

13. Sew buttons to first border at corners and center of each side.

MAKING A LABEL FOR YOUR QUILT

Make a separate label for your quilt from muslin or another light print fabric. Use a permanent fine marker for the lettering and signature. Turn raw edges to wrong side and hand stitch label to back of quilt.

Snowflake Design

PUMPKIN SEED QUILT

Approximate Size: 15" x 15"
Center Square: 7 1/2" x 7 1/2"

Materials & Supplies:

1/4 yd light fabric
1/2 yd dark fabric, first and third borders, binding and
   hanging tabs
1/8 yd light fabric, second border
1/2 yd each, backing fabric and batting
fabric marker
quilting thread, dark
between quilting needle
hoop or frame

Quilting Pattern (page 25):

Pumpkin Seed Design

Cutting Requirements:

8" x 8" square, light fabric
two 1 1/2" x 44" strips, dark fabric for first and third borders
three 2 1/4" x 44" strips, light fabric for second border
three 4" x 5" rectangles, dark fabric for hanging tabs
two 2" x 44" strips, dark fabric for binding
17" x 17" square, backing fabric
17" x 17" square, batting

Instructions:

Read pages 4 to 19 before beginning.

MAKING THE QUILT

1. Trace quilting design onto 8" light-colored fabric square using the fabric marker.

2. Sew first border to top and bottom edges first, then to sides. Repeat for second and third borders.

3. Layer, baste, and put the quilt into a hoop or frame.

4. Begin quilting the central motif with dark thread. Use the zigzag method of stitching, **Fig 1**, through the total pattern.

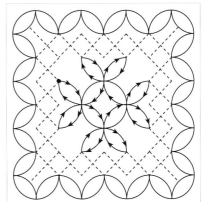

Fig 1

5. Quilt in the ditch, between each of the borders.

6. For hanging tabs, fold the 4" x 5" rectangles in half right sides together; stitch. Turn the tabs to the right side. Place one tab at the center of top edge of quilt with raw edges even; position remaining tabs in same manner about 3 1/4" from each side of center tab. Baste tabs in place.

ADDING THE BINDING

1. Place quilt on flat surface and trim backing and batting to the quilt top edge. Measure around the outside edges of the quilt. Join binding strips to that length.

2. Fold strip in half lengthwise with wrong sides together. Open the fold and make a long diagonal cut across the bias, **Fig 2**.

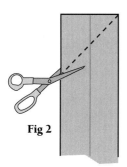

Fig 2

3. Fold down a 1/4" seam along the bias edge; refold strip lengthwise, **Fig 3**.

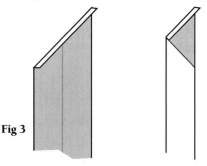

Fig 3

4. Place binding along the edge of the back of the quilted top with raw edges even; begin sewing along one side, **Fig 4**.

Fig 4

5. When you approach a corner, stitch to 1/4" from edge, **Fig 5A**. At the corner, fold the binding at a right angle away from the quilt top, **Fig 5B**; fold back so binding is even with next edge to be stitched, **Fig 5C**. Drop needle and continue sewing, **Fig 5D**. This right angle corner tuck will create a full mitered corner when turned to the right side and stitched down. Repeat at remaining corners.

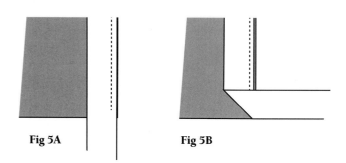

Fig 5A   **Fig 5B**

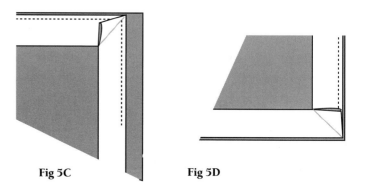

Fig 5C   **Fig 5D**

6. To finish end of binding, tuck raw end into the folded end at the beginning of the binding and finish sewing, **Fig 6**.

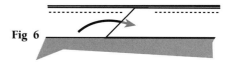

Fig 6

7. Turn binding to the right side of the quilt and stitch with a hidden slip stitch by hand. Close the mitered corner tuck with a few additional hand stitches.

MAKING A LABEL FOR YOUR QUILT

Make a separate label for your quilt from muslin or another light print fabric. Use a permanent fine marker for the lettering and signature. Turn raw edges to wrong side and hand stitch label to back of quilt.

Pumpkin Seed Design

AMISH STYLE QUILT

Approximate Size: 17" x 17"
Center square: 9" x 9"

Materials & Supplies:

1/3 yd green, center and corner stones
1/4 yd black, first border and binding
1/4 yd red, second border
5/8 yd each backing fabric and batting
fabric marker
freezer paper
posterboard or file folder
glue stick
black quilting thread
between needle
hoop or frame
freezer paper
ruler

Quilting Patterns (pages 28 and 29):

Feathered Wreath
Misshapen Heart
Feathered Border
Feathered Corner

Cutting Requirements:

9 1/2" x 9 1/2" center square, green
four 1 1/2" x 1 1/2" squares, green
four 4" x 4" squares, green
four 1 1/2" x 9 1/2" strips, black
four 4" x 11 1/2" strips, red
20" x 20" square backing fabric
two 2" x 44" strips, black for binding
20" x 20" square batting

Instructions

Read pages 4 to 19 before beginning.

MAKING A POSITIVE QUILTING STENCIL
1. Trace all Quilting Patterns onto tracing paper; glue to piece of file folder or poster board.

2. Cut out the patterns along outside edges. Cut small slits along the spine of the Feathered Wreath, **Fig 1**.

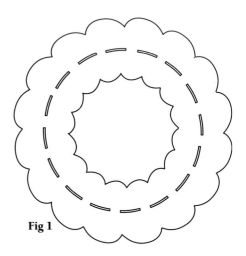

Fig 1

MARKING THE CENTER
1. Fold center fabric square in half diagonally and finger press. Fold along other diagonal and finger press. Center the feather stencil and pin or tape to the fabric. Using a fabric marker, mark the design onto the fabric; include open areas cut along the spine of the Feathered Wreath.

2. Using the Misshapen Heart stencil, mark all the feathers, **Fig 2**.

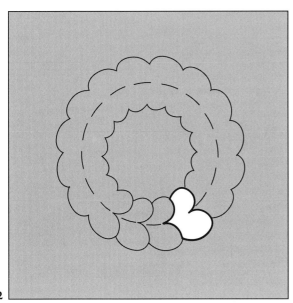

Fig 2

ASSEMBLING THE QUILT

1. Sew 1 1/2" x 9 1/2" black strips to top and bottom edge of center square. Sew 1 1/2" green square to each end of remaining two black strips; sew to sides of square.

2. Repeat step 1 with 4" x 11 1/2" red strips and 4" green squares.

3. For center square, draw a line outside Feathered Wreath along diagonal fold using a ruler and marking pen (or pencil). Draw another line 1/8" from the first line. Draw another pair of lines 1" from first pair. Continue drawing pairs of lines in same manner until entire background is filled in both directions, **Fig 3**.

4. Draw a 1/2" grid in center of Feathered Wreath, **Fig 3**.

Fig 3

MARKING THE BORDERS

One of the hallmarks of a fine hand quilter is reflected in the easy and natural transition of the border design around the corners of the quilt. The border shouldn't look awkward as it turns the corner. The border design for this quilt is the Feathered design. It is in two parts—the Feathered Border and Feathered Corner.

1. Place the Feathered Corner stencil on one of the quilt corners. The bottom of the vine should be just above the seam allowance; the lower feather in the corner stencil should drop down into the first border at the corner, **Fig 4**. Pin or tape the stencil down and mark around the design with the fabric marker. Repeat for remaining corners.

Fig 4

2. Place Feathered Border stencil between two of the marked corners; pin or tape stencil so that the ends match the corners. Mark the position of this stencil with the fabric marker. Repeat around the quilt.

FINISHING THE QUILT

1. Layer, baste and place quilt in a hoop.

2. Hand quilt the design starting in the middle and working outward. Quilt in the ditch of each edge of first border.

3. Trim quilt to 17" x 17".

MAKING THE HANGING SLEEVE

1. For the hanging sleeve, cut or tear an eight inch strip by the actual width of the quilt. Make a one inch hem at the ends of the strip.

2. Fold the long strip in half, wrong sides together, so that the halves are four inches wide; press the fold. Pin sleeve to back of quilt along top edge with raw edges even.

3. Sew binding to quilt (catching in the hanging sleeve strip) referring to Adding the Binding, page 22, in the Pumpkin Seed Quilt.

4. Tack lower edge of sleeve to back and batting of quilt without taking the stitches to the front of the quilt. Tack the back layer of the double sleeve to the quilt only at the ends. In this way a display pole will never touch the actual quilt back.

MAKING A LABEL FOR YOUR QUILT
Make a separate label for your quilt from muslin or another light print fabric. Use a permanent fine marker for the lettering and signature. Turn raw edges to wrong side and hand stitch label to back of quilt.

Feathered Border

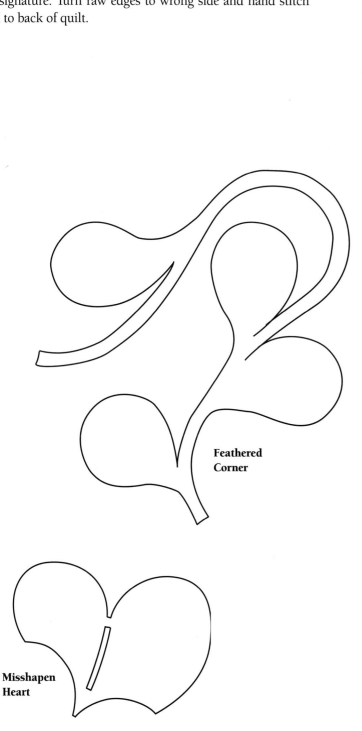

Feathered Corner

Misshapen Heart

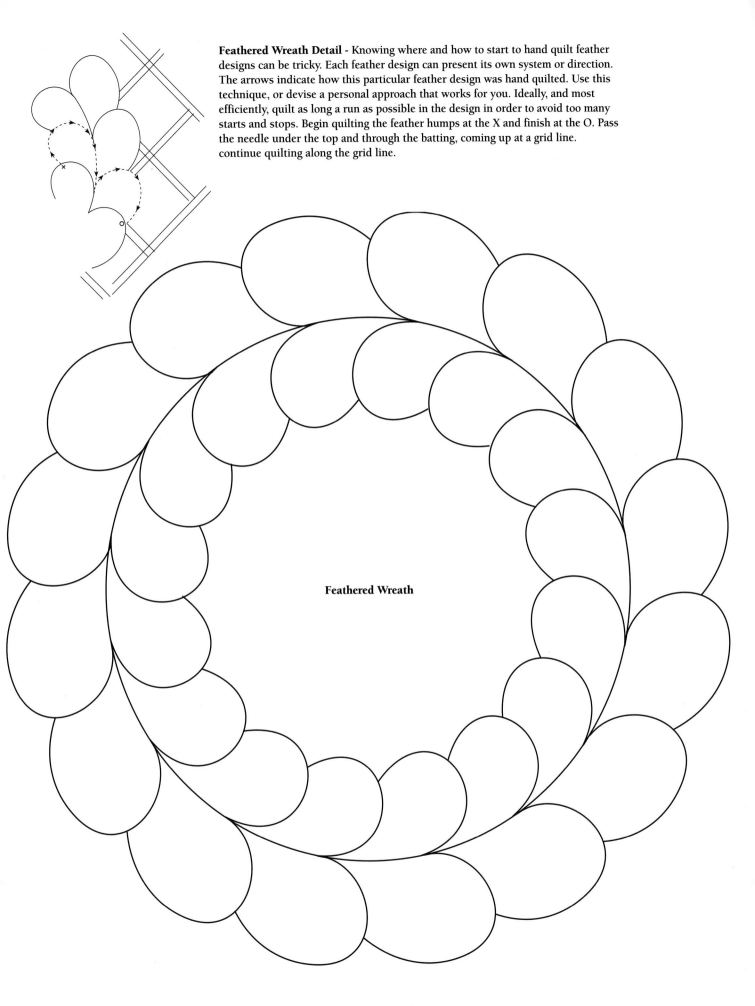

Feathered Wreath Detail - Knowing where and how to start to hand quilt feather designs can be tricky. Each feather design can present its own system or direction. The arrows indicate how this particular feather design was hand quilted. Use this technique, or devise a personal approach that works for you. Ideally, and most efficiently, quilt as long a run as possible in the design in order to avoid too many starts and stops. Begin quilting the feather humps at the X and finish at the O. Pass the needle under the top and through the batting, coming up at a grid line. continue quilting along the grid line.

Feathered Wreath

WELCOME QUILT WITH WHEAT AND PINEAPPLE

Approximate Size: 27" x 27"
Center square: 18" x 18"

Materials & Supplies:

5/8 yd peach solid, center and second border
1/8 yd red print, cornerstones
1/2 yd blue print, first border, cornerstones and binding
1 yd each backing fabric and batting
fabric marker
freezer paper
quilting thread
between needle
hoop or frame
yardstick

Cutting Requirements:

one 18 1/2" x 18 1/2" peach square, center
four 5" x 22 1/2" strips peach, second border
four 2" x 2" squares red, cornerstones
two 2" x 44" strips blue, first border
four 5" x 5" blue squares, corner stones
four 2" x 44" strips blue, binding

34" x 34" square each, backing fabric and batting
two 3 1/2" x 12 1/2" pieces freezer paper
one 4" x 4" square freezer paper
craft knife

Quilting Patterns (pages 31 to 33):

Pineapple and Wheat
Feathered Wreath
Border Wheat Stalk
Border Square Wheat

Instructions

Read pages 4 to 19 before beginning.

MAKING THE QUILT

1. Trace Pineapple and Wheat quilting pattern onto paper; trace Feathered Wreath around Pineapple and Wheat.

2. Center the 18 1/2" peach square on top of the traced quilting design. Using a light box or another light source behind the copy, trace the design onto the fabric.

3. Tape the fabric square to a table top. Using a yardstick, mark the background one inch grid. Lay the yard stick on the diagonal from corner to corner to mark the first line. The second line should be the line diagonally from the opposite corners. Continue to mark the diagonal grid at 1" intervals by moving the yardstick along the diagonals.

4. Mark the center of the Pineapple and Wheat grid in 1/4" increments.

5. Sew the 2" blue print border strips to opposite sides of center square.

6. Sew 2" red square to each end of remaining two blue print strips; sew to remaining sides of center square.

7. Repeat steps 5 and 6 with 5"-wide peach strips and 5" blue print squares.

8. For the border, make negative space stencils. Trace the Border Wheat Stalk design onto one of the 3 1/2" x 12 1/2" pieces of freezer paper. Layer the two pieces of freezer paper with the shiny sides together; pin paper together at each end. Cut out areas of grain and stalk with a craft knife, protecting your table with a rotary mat or heavy cardboard. Unpin the papers to find the necessary mirror images for the wheat border.

9. Trace and cut out Border Square Wheat design from 4" square of freezer paper.

10. Place the two Wheat Stalk stencils along one peach border close to the first border—they will overlap at the stems. When you are pleased with the arrangement, pin one of the wheat strips in place. Press the freezer paper down with a dry iron. *Note: You will be able to pick up and move the stencil if it is not quite right.* Mark the design with the marker when the fabric is cool. Add viny stems between and at tips of leaves. Iron the opposite Wheat Stalk design in place and repeat the process.

11. Place the Border Square Wheat design where stalks overlap; mark design. Refer to photograph on front cover for placement.

12. Repeat steps 10 and 11 for the remaining three sides.

Hint: Iron the freezer paper to a file folder and cut the design out with a craft knife if you find the freezer paper to be too flimsy for tracing.

13. Layer, baste, and put the quilt into a hoop or frame.

14. Hand quilt the design beginning with the central motif and working outward.

15. Make a hanging sleeve referring to Making a Hanging Sleeve, page 27, in the Amish Quilt.

16. Bind the quilt referring to Adding the Binding, page 24, in the Pumpkin Seed Quilt.

MAKING A LABEL FOR YOUR QUILT
Make a separate label for your quilt from muslin or another light print fabric. Use a permanent fine marker for the lettering and signature. Turn raw edges to wrong side and hand stitch label to back of quilt.

Border Square Wheat

Border Wheat Stalk

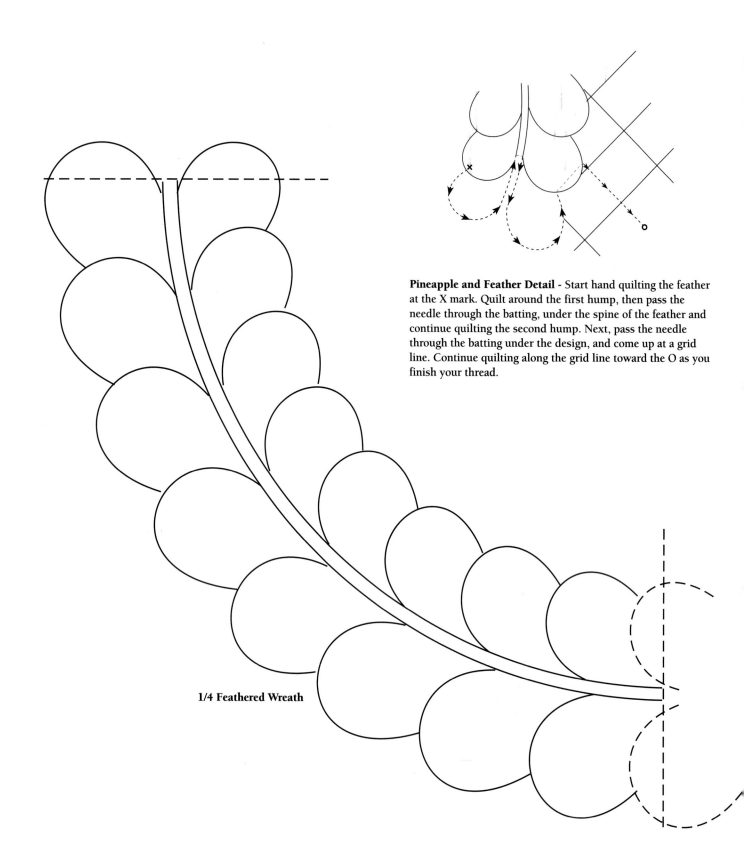

Pineapple and Feather Detail - Start hand quilting the feather at the X mark. Quilt around the first hump, then pass the needle through the batting, under the spine of the feather and continue quilting the second hump. Next, pass the needle through the batting under the design, and come up at a grid line. Continue quilting along the grid line toward the O as you finish your thread.

1/4 Feathered Wreath

Pineapple and Wheat

produced by Rita Weiss